COLOUR HISTORY

Welcome to the world of Colour History. A book of fun and learning where children can colour in scenes from Britain's colourful past. Then read and learn about the events of the time.

Bring history to life in the fourth of the Colour History series.

Book Four Contents

Written and Illustrated by Les Ives

Published by Colour History Ltd

DICK TURPIN

Richard "Dick" Turpin was born in 1705 in Essex. He trained as a butcher, but soon turned to crime.

In these days the countryside was full of gangs of men called poachers, who would roam local estates stealing animals. Turpin bought the stolen animals and sold the meat in his shop.

Eventually Turpin joined one of these gangs and began to take part in violent raids on country houses. After a series of robberies some gang members were caught and hanged.

Turpin escaped to Kent where he became a "highwayman". He would lie in wait on quiet country roads attacking and robbing passing coaches. He soon became well known and decided to move to Yorkshire. He gave himself a new name, John Palmer, and became a horse trader.

Most of the horses he sold were stolen and people became suspicious of the stranger. Eventually he was arrested and was taken to York and accused of horse stealing.

Turpin then made a terrible mistake. He wrote to his family in Essex, but they would not accept his letter. The letter found its way into the hands of Turpin's old school teacher, James Smith. He recognised his former pupil's handwriting as that of the famous highwayman, Dick Turpin.

After being found guilty of his crimes Dick Turpin was hanged in York on April 7, 1739.

Funny Fact

One very poor highwayman could not afford a gun and successfully held-up a coach with a candlestick!

Dick Turpin
holds-up a coach

CAPTAIN COOK

James Cook was born in 1728 in Marton-in-Cleveland. He moved to Whitby in North Yorkshire, where he trained to become a sailor.

The eighteenth century was an age of exploration and the Royal Society wanted to explore the vast unknown areas of the Pacific Ocean. Captain Cook was chosen to make the voyage, as he was a skillful sailor and an expert navigator and mapmaker.

He left Plymouth harbour in his ship the "Endeavour" in 1768. During his three-year trip, Cook discovered New Zealand and the East coast of Australia. On his second voyage he travelled to the Southern Pacific. The scientists on board ship brought back to England animals and plants, which had never been seen before in Europe.

Cook was a fair and caring captain. His men were fed on fruit and vegetables, which kept them free of "scurvy", the dreaded disease, that often struck sailors in those days.

His final voyage in 1776 was to find a safe passage around Canada and Alaska, but disaster struck. Captain Cook and his ship the "Resolution", sailed into the Hawaiian Islands and a minor dispute with local tribesmen resulted in him being killed on the beach.

Captain Cook's crew completed the trip, but England had lost its greatest explorer of the seas.

Funny Fact

On reaching Madeira 3,000 gallons of wine added to the huge amounts of provisions already on board. This gave Captain Cook's one- handed chef more than a handful of problems!

Captain Cook discovers
New Zealand

LORD NELSON

Horatio Nelson was born in 1758 the son of a village rector in Norfolk.

He joined the navy as a young man and saw action against the Spanish in Latin America. He was given his own ship by the age of twenty.

In France, Napoleon Bonaparte had risen to power and soon the British were at war with their old enemy. Nelson was wounded in action at Toulon and lost his right eye, but despite this he continued to climb the ranks.

Nelson's first major victory was at St. Vincent against the Spanish. He was badly wounded again, shortly afterwards losing his right arm. He recovered and went on to crush the French at the Battle of the Nile in Egypt.

In 1805 Napoleon was determined to invade England and he managed to raise an enormous French and Spanish fleet. Nelson sailed to face them and a ferocious battle took place at Cape Trafalgar.

Whilst he was standing on the deck of his famous flagship, the "Victory", Nelson was shot by a sniper in a French ship. Nelson was taken below deck, but died later of his wounds.

His brilliant planning and the superior English ships won an historic victory. The French fleet was destroyed and Napoleon's plans to invade Britain lay in ruins.

Nelson was responsible for improving the life and conditions for his sailors. He also established Britain as a great sea power for the next one hundred years.

Funny Fact

Food on board Nelson's ships was not good. The cheese was so hard that the sailors were able to carve hard-wearing buttons for their jackets!

Lord Nelson on the deck
of HMS Victory

DUKE OF WELLINGTON

Arthur Wesley, later the Duke of Wellington, was born into a noble family in Dublin in 1769.

He joined the army at the age of eighteen and quickly rose to the rank of Colonel. He made his name fighting in India and won a famous victory at the battle of Assaye. He was respected for the care he took of his soldiers.

The Emperor of France, Napoleon Bonaparte, had started a war in Europe. After many years of conquest, he invaded Portugal and Wesley led the British army to face the French. The war became known as the "Peninsular War".

Wesley proved to be a brilliant General and after crushing defeats at Salamanca and Vitoria, the French fled back to France. Napoleon was defeated and Wesley returned home to be made the Duke of Wellington.

The French Emperor was exiled but returned in 1815. He raised an army and marched into Belgium. Wellington and his allied army faced Napoleon on the field of Waterloo. A bloodthirsty battle followed and Napoleon was finally defeated.

The Duke of Wellington was less successful in later life. His time spent in politics and as Prime Minister was often difficult, as the country went through a period of great social change.

However, when he died in 1852 he was given a state funeral and was buried in St Paul's Cathedral.

Funny Fact

Some of the earliest sets of false teeth were made from the teeth of the dead soldiers found on the battlefield of Waterloo!

The Duke of Wellington at
the battle of Waterloo

QUEEN VICTORIA

Victoria became Queen of England in 1837 at the age of eighteen. Her reign lasted for sixty-four years and during that time, Britain underwent one of its greatest periods of change.

During the early years of her reign Victoria had the guidance of her Prime Minister, Lord Melbourne. She married the German Prince Albert, in 1840.

Britain's industries were amongst the most powerful in the world. Mills, coalmines, ironworks and shipyards covered the country. Britain's industrial power created great wealth for the country, although many of the workers who lived in the towns endured terrible health and poverty.

The Empire abroad continued to grow and prosper and included Canada, India, Australia, New Zealand and large colonies in Africa and the Far East. The Great Exhibition at Crystal Palace in 1851 was a celebration of Britain's greatness.

Major progress was made in medicine and science. The discovery of electricity, telephones and recorded sound were major advances.

Victoria's life was shattered in 1861 when her beloved Albert died. The Queen mourned her loss in her Scottish castle at Balmoral many miles away from her subjects in London.

The colourful new Prime Minster, Benjamin Disraeli, eventually persuaded her to re-enter public life. Queen Victoria celebrated her Diamond Jubilee, before her death in 1901.

Funny Fact

For 50 years Queen Victoria drew the blinds when passing Newcastle on her train. She vowed never to look upon the town again, as the manager of a hotel there had once presented her with a bill for a banquet!

Queen Victoria in her royal carriage

FLORENCE NIGHTINGALE

Florence Nightingale was born in 1820 and spent many of her early years in Derbyshire. She was well educated and became a trained nurse.

Florence was a religious woman and in 1837 she believed she had heard the voice of God telling her that she had a mission.

In 1853 the Crimean war broke out, with Britain and France fighting against the Russians over land in the Balkans. The war was very bloody, and the people of Britain expressed their horror at the suffering of the wounded soldiers.

Florence and a small group of nurses were sent to an army hospital in Turkey. The wards were full of rats and fleas and there was very little clean water. Many of the men slept on straw in the hospital corridors.

She immediately ordered the cleaning of the wards and the soldiers' clothes to be washed. She did not allow other nurses into the wards at night, but made her ward rounds alone, giving comfort and advice. The soldiers called her "The Lady of the Lamp".

Through her work, all of the Crimean hospitals were improved and she returned to England a heroine.

She continued her work through the Army Medical School and the Nightingale School for Nurses. In later years she did a lot to improve the life and health of people in the Victorian workhouses.

After a lifetime of good work, Florence Nightingale died in 1910.

Funny Fact

Although Florence improved the nursing care in hospitals, doctors often operated in their Sunday best clothes!

Florence Nightingale
making her ward rounds

GRACE DARLING

Grace Darling was born in 1815 in Northumberland. Her father, William, was the keeper of the Longstone Lighthouse, off the Farne Islands.

Grace was an ordinary girl and very few people could have guessed that she would become one of the most famous heroines in the world.

Early in the morning of 7th September 1838, the Darling family were awoken by a ferocious storm. Looking out to sea, Grace could see that a ship had run aground on the Big Harcar Rock about a mile away.

The "Forfarshire" had set sail from Hull bound for Dundee. She carried a valuable cargo, passengers and crew. Through her telescope Grace could see survivors clinging to the stricken ship.

Grace persuaded her father that they could row out and rescue the survivors. The lighthouse boat, called a coble, was lowered into the raging North Sea. The little flat-bottomed boat was pushed off course many times, but eventually they reached the terrified survivors.

Five of the nine survivors were rescued on their first trip. William Darling and two of the rescued seamen managed to save another four. It was three days before anyone could leave the safety of the lighthouse.

Sadly, Grace died of tuberculosis four years later in 1842.

Funny Fact

The Eider ducks of the Farne Islands are so tame that they have been known to make their nests in houses and sometimes under people's beds!

Grace Darling bravely
rows to the sinking ship

CHARLES DICKENS

Charles Dickens was born in 1812 and grew up in Kent and London. His happy childhood ended abruptly when his father was put in prison because of his debts. Dickens was forced to leave school and work in a shoe polish factory.

Eventually he became a clerk and then a court reporter. His love of writing grew and he started to write his own stories. His work soon began to be published.

He wrote a series of novels including many children's stories such as "A Christmas Carol" and comic tales like "The Pickwick Papers" and "Nicholas Nickleby". Dickens wrote historical stories such as "A Tale of Two Cities" and "Barnaby Rudge". The public loved them all.

He was a thoughtful and caring man and books such as "Oliver Twist" and "Great Expectations", went a long way in portraying the social problems of Victorian Britain.

His fame became worldwide and he often travelled to America to give readings of his books. With his long hair and stylish clothes he was a popular and colourful figure.

Sadly, the long hours of work and travel began to affect his health and he died, whilst writing the novel "The Mystery of Edwin Drood" in 1870.

Funny Fact

Wackford Squeers in Nicholas Nickleby was based on a real-life headmaster from Bowes!

Dickens wrote about
Victorian life

DR LIVINGSTONE

David Livingstone was born into a very poor family in Blantyre, Scotland in 1813.

In 1834 the Church of Scotland was training missionaries to send to poorer countries. After studying for two years in Glasgow, Livingstone was sent to Africa.

He began his adventures at Kuraman on the Cape frontier and soon he had travelled further than any other white man before him. He encountered many dangers and was even attacked by a lion!

He briefly came home to get married, but soon returned to Africa. With a small band of native helpers, he travelled through Zambezi and Mozambique. He discovered and named the Victoria Falls after Queen Victoria.

He returned to England in 1856, and was hailed a national hero.

After several more trips, Livingstone began his final expedition in 1866. He wanted to explore the East coast of Africa, spread Christianity and help to end the evil slave trade. It was a long and difficult journey and Livingstone became quite ill. Many of his helpers deserted him.

The American journalist, Henry Stanley, joined him on part of the journey and they managed to travel as far as the start of the Congo River. By now Livingstone was growing weaker, but Stanley could not persuade him to return home.

Dr Livingstone's health grew poor and he eventually died in Zambia in 1873.

Funny Fact

Victorian travellers could look forward to a unique cure for travel sickness in foreign lands. It was suggested that they mix gunpowder in a glass of warm soapy water and drink it!

Livingstone discovers
the Victoria falls

1. **Balmoral Castle** - Queen Victoria spent many years here.

2. **Glasgow** - Dr Livingstone's home town.

3. **Northumberland** - Site of the Longstone Lighthouse scene of Grace Darling's brave rescue.

4. **Marton-in-Cleveland** - Captain Cook's birthplace.

5. **Whitby** - The town where Captain Cook undertook his sailing apprenticeship.

6. **Manchester** - Many Victorian mills were built in this northern town.

7. **Ireland** - Thousands of Irish people came to work in England.

8. **York** - Dick Turpin was hanged in York.

9. **Wales** - Famous for its mining in Victorian times.

10. **Derbyshire** - Florence Nightingale grew up here.

11. **Norfolk** - Birthplace of Lord Nelson.

12. **Bristol** - A famous railway was built from London to Bristol.

13. **Crystal Palace** - Site of the famous National Exhibition.

14. **Kent** - Dick Turpin robbed many people in Kent.

15. **Kent** - Charles Dickens grew up in Kent and London.

16. **Plymouth** - Captain Cook set sail on many famous voyages from this port.

17. **Portsmouth** - Nelson sailed from Portsmouth to defeat the French at Trafalgar.

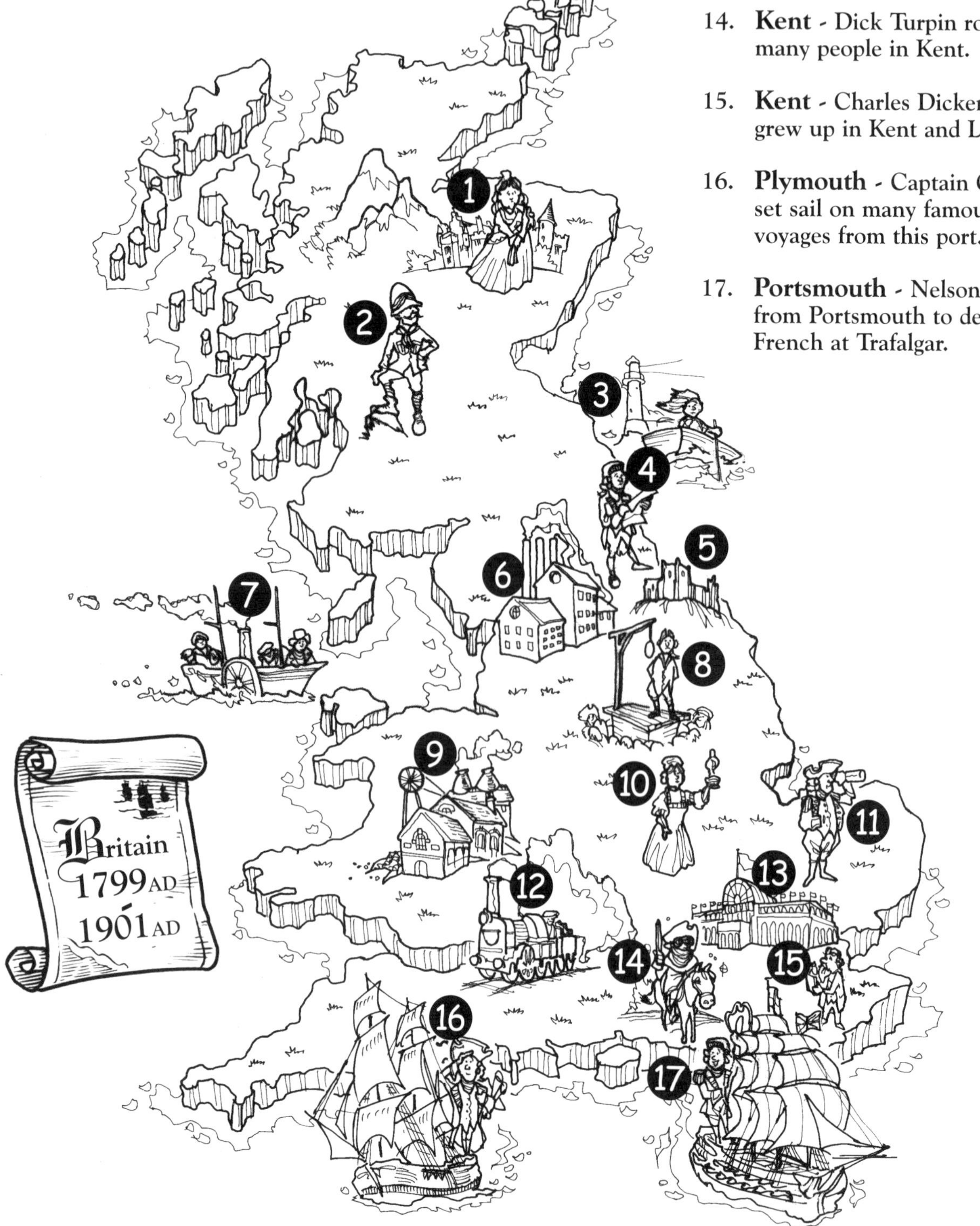